The Holy Spirit
Under the Influence

STUDY GUIDE
by Edith Bajema

Grand Rapids, Michigan

We thank Edith Bajema of Grand Rapids, Michigan, for writing this study.

Unless otherwise indicated, the Scripture quotations in this publication are from the HOLY BIBLE, NEW INTERNATIONAL VERSION, © 1973, 1978, 1984, International Bible Society. Used by permission of Zondervan Bible Publishers.

Discover Life series. The Holy Spirit: Under the Influence, © 1997 by Faith Alive Christian Resources, 2850 Kalamazoo Ave. SE, Grand Rapids, MI 49560. All rights reserved. With the exception of brief excerpts for review purposes, no part of this book may be reproduced in any manner whatsoever without written permission from the publisher. Printed in the United States of America. 1-800-333-8300 (US).

ISBN 978-1-56212-583-7

10 9 8 7 6 5 4 3

Contents

Introduction

Lesson 1: The Spirit Poured Out

Lesson 2: New Life in the Spirit

Lesson 3: The Spirit as Our Counselor

Lesson 4: The Spirit's Sword

Lesson 5: The Spirit of Holiness

Lesson 6: The Spirit of Power

Lesson 7: The Gifts of the Spirit

Evaluation

Introduction

The Holy Spirit: Under the Influence introduces us to God the Holy Spirit. Although the Spirit's work may seem less visible to us than that of God the Father and God the Son, it is absolutely essential to our well-being. Without it we cannot, and will not, benefit from the saving work of Jesus Christ.

The Holy Spirit is the life-giver. When God calls the universe into being, it is the Spirit who "hovers over the surface of the deep" (Genesis 1:2), breathing order and life into the primordial chaos. And just as the Holy Spirit gives physical life, so the Spirit grants us eternal life in Jesus Christ (John 3:5).

It is the Holy Spirit who connects us with the saving, re-creating, regenerating, invigorating work of Christ. Our risen, ascended Lord is in heaven. There God the Father has given him all authority and power. The Spirit provides us with a lifeline to Jesus by which we may receive his power even while we are still living here below. Through the gift to us of this heaven-sent Comforter, we can become already in this life much of what we will one day be in fullness.

Through the indwelling of God's Spirit—God *in* us—we are united with Christ—God *with* us. The Spirit unites us with Christ and with his heavenly power through the gift of faith. Faith brings into our lives the process of sanctification, of becoming more and more pure and perfect like Jesus and increasingly devoted to the service of God and each other.

Before Jesus ascended to heaven God's Spirit was already present on the earth, giving and sustaining human life and granting godly wisdom to some, most notably to Jesus himself. The Spirit also sprinkled faith and spiritual gifts among a number of God's chosen Old Testament people. But the Spirit's saving activity was confined more or less to the nation of Israel. It is not until Jesus' ascension that the Spirit is poured out in fullness upon people of every race, tribe, and nation.

On the day of Pentecost the saving power of God that the Spirit brings begins to flood the whole world, spilling over every boundary that prevents people from hearing and believing the Good News of salvation through Jesus' death and resurrection. As the seven sessions of *The Holy Spirit: Under the Influence* demonstrate, we truly live not in the Age of Aquarius but in the Age of the Spirit. It is to a deeper understanding of the practical, everyday presence of God's Spirit in our lives that this study guides us. It allows us to search the Scriptures to see the wonders that God is doing all over the world—and right within our very own souls.

STUDY GUIDE

The Spirit Poured Out
Lesson 1

John 7:37-39

³⁷On the last and greatest day of the Feast, Jesus stood and said in a loud voice, "If anyone is thirsty, let him come to me and drink. ³⁸Whoever believes in me, as the Scripture has said, streams of living water will flow from within him." ³⁹By this he meant the Spirit, whom those who believed in him were later to receive. Up to that time the Spirit had not been given, since Jesus had not yet been glorified.

Acts 1:4-5, 8-9

⁴On one occasion, while he was eating with them, [Jesus] gave [the apostles he had chosen] this command: "Do not leave Jerusalem, but wait for the gift my Father promised, which you have heard me speak about. ⁵For John baptized with water, but in a few days you will be baptized with the Holy Spirit. . . .

⁸"But you will receive power when the Holy Spirit comes on you; and you will be my witnesses in Jerusalem, and in all Judea and Samaria, and to the ends of the earth."

⁹After he said this, he was taken up before their very eyes, and a cloud hid him from their sight.

Acts 2:1-8, 11-18

¹When the day of Pentecost came, they were all together in one place. ²Suddenly a sound like the blowing of a violent wind came from heaven and filled the whole house where they were sitting. ³They saw what seemed to be tongues of fire that separated and came to rest on each of them. ⁴All of them were filled with the Holy Spirit and began to speak in other tongues as the Spirit enabled them.

⁵Now there were staying in Jerusalem God-fearing Jews from every nation under heaven. ⁶When they heard this sound, a crowd came together in bewilderment, because each one heard them speaking in his own language. ⁷Utterly amazed, they asked: "Are not all these men who are speaking Galileans? ⁸Then how is it that each of us hears them in his own native language? . . . ¹¹We hear them declaring the wonders of God in our own tongues!" ¹²Amazed and perplexed, they asked one another, "What does this mean?"

¹³Some, however, made fun of them and said, "They have had too much wine."

¹⁴Then Peter stood up with the Eleven, raised his voice and addressed the crowd: "Fellow Jews and all of you who live in Jerusalem, let me explain this to you; listen carefully to what I say. ¹⁵These men are not drunk, as you suppose. It's only nine in the morning! ¹⁶No, this is what was spoken by the prophet Joel:

¹⁷"'In the last days, God says,
  I will pour out my Spirit on all people.
Your sons and daughters will prophesy,
  your young men will see visions,
  your old men will dream dreams.
¹⁸Even on my servants, both men and women,
  I will pour out my Spirit in those days,
  and they will prophesy.'"

Acts 10:36, 43-46

³⁶"You know the message God sent to the people of Israel, telling the good news of peace through Jesus Christ, who is Lord of all . . .

⁴³"All the prophets testify about him that everyone who believes in him receives forgiveness of sins through his name."

⁴⁴While Peter was still speaking these words, the Holy Spirit came on all who heard the message. ⁴⁵The circumcised believers who had come with Peter were astonished that the gift of the Holy Spirit had been poured out even on the Gentiles. ⁴⁶For they heard them speaking in tongues and praising God.

Questions

1. Why is it so hard to wait for something that you eagerly anticipate?

2. **John 7:37-39**
   a. How does Jesus describe the Holy Spirit to his listeners?
   b. When he speaks to them at the feast, has the Spirit been given to them yet? Why or why not?

3. **Acts 1:4-5, 8-9**
   a. What gift has the Father promised to Jesus' followers?
   b. What will they receive when the Spirit comes upon them? What will they become?
   c. What happens to Jesus after he speaks with his followers?

4. **Acts 2:1-8, 11-18**
   a. Describe what the believers hear and see on Pentecost. What do they begin to do?
   b. Who hears the commotion? What do they think?
   c. How does Peter explain what has happened?
   d. According to the prophet Joel, what happens when God pours out his Spirit on all people?

5. **Acts 10:36, 43-46**
   a. What message does Peter preach?
   b. What happens as he preaches?
   c. How does Peter know that the Spirit has been poured out on his listeners?

Summary

a. What new things did you learn about the Holy Spirit in this lesson?

b. What seems to accompany the Spirit's coming?

STUDIES IN THIS SERIES

- Lesson 1: The Spirit Poured Out
- Lesson 2: New Life in the Spirit
- Lesson 3: The Spirit as Our Counselor
- Lesson 4: The Spirit's Sword
- Lesson 5: The Spirit of Holiness
- Lesson 6: The Spirit of Power
- Lesson 7: The Gifts of the Spirit

afterWord

Heavenly Dove

When Nansen started on his Arctic Expedition he took a carrier pigeon. After two years of desolation in the Arctic region, he wrote a message, tied it to the pigeon's wing, and let it loose to travel two thousand miles to Norway. Imagine it—one tiny bird making a journey of two thousand miles. Finally, the bird flew into the lap of Nansen's wife in Norway. She knew, by the arrival of the bird, that all was well in the dark night of the North. So, with the coming of the Holy Spirit, the Heavenly Dove, the disciples knew that Christ was alive, for the Spirit's coming and manifestation of power were proofs of that fact.

—G. CURTIS JONES IN *1000 ILLUSTRATIONS FOR PREACHING AND TEACHING*

The Power to Pump

A. J. Gordon, one of the founders of Gordon Conwell Divinity School, told of being out walking and looking across a field at a house. There beside the house was what looked like a man pumping furiously at one of those hand pumps. As Gordon watched, the man continued to pump up and down, without ever slowing in the slightest, much less stopping.

Truly it was a remarkable sight, so Gordon started to walk toward it. As he got closer, he could see it was not a man at the pump, but a wooden figure painted to look like a man. The arm that was pumping so rapidly was hinged at the elbow and the hand was wired to the pump handle. The water was pouring forth, but not because the figure was pumping it. You see, it was an artesian well, and the water was pumping the man!

When you see a man who is at work for God and producing results, recognize that it is the Holy Spirit working through him, not the man's efforts that are giving results. All he has to do—and all you have to do—is keep your hand on the handle.

—*ILLUSTRATIONS FOR BIBLICAL PREACHING*, MICHAEL P. GREEN, ED.

Songmaker of the Trinity

Dancing with no music is tough stuff.

Jesus knew that. For that reason, on the night before His death He introduced the disciples to the songmaker of the Trinity, the Holy Spirit. "When I go away, I will send the Helper to you. If I do not go away, the Helper will not come. When the Helper comes, he will prove to the people of the world the truth about sin, about being right with God, and about judgment" (John 16:7-8, NCV).

If I were to ask you to describe your heavenly Father, you'd give me a response. If I were to ask you to tell me what Jesus did for you, you'd likely give a cogent answer. But if I were to ask about the role of the Holy Spirit in your life ... eyes would duck. Throats would be cleared. And it would soon be obvious that of the three persons of the Godhead, the Holy Spirit is the one we understand the least.

Perhaps the most common mistake regarding the Spirit is perceiving Him as power and not a person, a force with no identity. Such is not true. The Holy Spirit is a person. "The world cannot accept him, because it does not see him or know him. But you know him, because he lives with you and he will be in you" (John 14:17, NCV).

The Holy Spirit is not an "it." He is a person. He has knowledge (1 Corinthians 2:11). He has a will (1 Corinthians 12:11). He has a mind (Romans 8:27). He has affections (Romans 15:30). You can lie to Him (Acts 5:3-4). You can insult Him (Hebrews 10:29). You can grieve Him (Ephesians 4:30).

The Holy Spirit is not an impersonal force. He is not Popeye's spinach or the surfer's wave. He is God within you to help you. In fact John calls Him the Helper.

Envision a father helping his son learn to ride a bicycle, and you will have a partial picture of the Holy Spirit. The father stays at the son's side. He pushes the bike and steadies it if the boy starts to tumble. The Spirit does that for us; He stays our step and strengthens our stride. Unlike the father, however, He never leaves. He is with us to the end of the age.

—MAX LUCADO IN *DISCIPLESHIP JOURNAL*, JANUARY/FEBRUARY 1996

As Living Epistles

Christ is expecting us to bring glory to his name and we are so often a stumbling block both to the world and to our fellow believers, simply because we lack power from on high!

God needs today not so much inspired apostles as living epistles known and read of all men. Just as God's written Word was inspired by the Holy Spirit, so must the "living epistle" of today be inspired by the self-same Spirit. As Christ overcame by the power of the Holy Spirit, so also must we (Revelation 3:21).

—ANONYMOUS

Gathered

At Pentecost the Holy Spirit
was given to the church.
In pouring his Spirit on many
  peoples
God overcomes the divisions of
  Babel;
now people from every tongue, tribe,
  and nation
are gathered into the unity
of the body of Christ.

—*OUR WORLD BELONGS TO GOD*, STANZA 30

STUDY GUIDE

New Life in the Spirit
Lesson 2

John 3:3-8
³Jesus declared, "I tell you the truth, no one can see the kingdom of God unless he is born again."

⁴"How can a man be born when he is old?" Nicodemus asked. "Surely he cannot enter a second time into his mother's womb to be born!"

⁵Jesus answered, "I tell you the truth, no one can enter the kingdom of God unless he is born of water and the Spirit. ⁶Flesh gives birth to flesh, but the Spirit gives birth to spirit. ⁷You should not be surprised at my saying, 'You must be born again.' ⁸The wind blows wherever it pleases. You hear its sound, but you cannot tell where it comes from or where it is going. So it is with everyone born of the Spirit."

Romans 7:5-6
⁵For when we were controlled by the sinful nature, the sinful passions aroused by the law were at work in our bodies, so that we bore fruit for death. ⁶But now, by dying to what once bound us, we have been released from the law so that we serve in the new way of the Spirit, and not in the old way of the written code.

Galatians 3:2-3, 5
²I would like to learn just one thing from you: Did you receive the Spirit by observing the law, or by believing what you heard? ³Are you so foolish? After beginning with the Spirit, are you now trying to attain your goal by human effort? . . . ⁵Does God give you his Spirit and work miracles among you because you observe the law, or because you believe what you heard?

Romans 8:1-6
¹Therefore, there is now no condemnation for those who are in Christ Jesus, ²because through Christ Jesus the law of the Spirit of life set me free from the law of sin and death. ³For what the law was powerless to do in that it was weakened by the sinful nature, God did by sending his own Son in the likeness of sinful man to be a sin offering. And so he condemned sin in sinful man, ⁴in order that the righteous requirements of the law might be fully met in us, who do not live according to the sinful nature but according to the Spirit.

⁵Those who live according to the sinful nature have their minds set on what that nature desires; but those who live in accordance with the Spirit have their minds set on what the Spirit desires. ⁶The mind of sinful man is death, but the mind controlled by the Spirit is life and peace.

Romans 8:11-16
¹¹And if the Spirit of him who raised Jesus from the dead is living in you, he who raised Christ from the dead will also give life to your mortal bodies through his Spirit, who lives in you.

¹²Therefore, brothers, we have an obligation—but it is not to the sinful nature, to live according to it. ¹³For if you live according to the sinful nature, you will die; but if by the Spirit you put to death the misdeeds of the body, you will live, ¹⁴because those who are led by the Spirit of God are sons of God. ¹⁵For you did not receive a spirit that makes you a slave again to fear, but you received the Spirit of sonship. And by him we cry, "Abba, Father." ¹⁶The Spirit himself testifies with our spirit that we are God's children.

Questions
1. Which of the following would you say best describes the change that takes place when one becomes a Christian: (1) accepting a new set of religious beliefs, (2) trying to live by a different moral standard, or (3) becoming an entirely new person? Explain.

2. **John 3:3-8**
   a. According to Jesus, how can anyone see or enter the kingdom of God?
   b. What is new, or born again, when someone enters the kingdom of God?
   c. Is this a process we can see, or is it invisible? Explain.

3. **Romans 7:5-6**
   a. Do you ever struggle with wanting to do something once you're told not to do it? Explain.
   b. Why do you think we can't serve God perfectly under the old system of the law?
   c. How is "the new way of the Spirit" different from "the old way of the written code"?

4. **Galatians 3:2-3, 5**
   a. How did the Galatian believers receive the Spirit?
   b. What have they forgotten, and what are they trying to do as a result?
   c. What do these verses tell you about new life in the Spirit?

5. **Romans 8:1-6**
   a. Why is there no condemnation for those who are in Christ Jesus?
   b. How did God take care of the law's requirements?
   c. What is the difference between "those who live according to the sinful nature" and "those who live in accordance with the Spirit"?

6. **Romans 8:11-16**
   a. What promise does God make to those who have the Holy Spirit living in them?
   b. How should they live?
   c. What assurance does the Spirit bring?

Summary
How would you describe the kind of change that the Spirit brings to a person's life?

STUDIES IN THIS SERIES
Lesson 1: The Spirit Poured Out
Lesson 2: New Life in the Spirit
Lesson 3: The Spirit as Our Counselor
Lesson 4: The Spirit's Sword
Lesson 5: The Spirit of Holiness
Lesson 6: The Spirit of Power
Lesson 7: The Gifts of the Spirit

afterWord

Pearl Divers

The pearl diver lives at the bottom of the ocean by means of the pure air conveyed to him from above. His life is entirely dependent on the breath from above him. We are down here, like the diver, to gather pearls for our Master's crown. The source of our life comes from the life-giving Spirit.

—HENRY DRUMMOND

Surrender— The Key to Power

The power of God is experienced through an act of personal surrender. [God's power] is different from other powers, whether material, social, or spiritual. The power of God cannot be controlled by human beings. Paul speaks of it as the power of the cross (1 Corinthians 1:17). Only by going through a process of dying to self and surrendering one's life to God can we have any hope of experiencing the power of God....

The power of God is available only to those who surrender their life and will to Him, and allow themselves to go where He leads them, and do what He wants them to do. We become faucets for His living water, earthen vessels for Him to use. We do not "control" or "use" the power of God. The power of God is thus different from all other powers at the center of every worldview. God controls us. We do not control Him.

In my second year of ministry, I was profoundly disillusioned with my faith in rational power. I was ready to surrender my life to God; in my self-surrender, I asked Jesus to baptize me with His Spirit. The resulting experience of God's love, joy, peace and power flowed from that prayer of relinquishment. In recent years, however, many "charismatic" people have asked for the Holy Spirit for personal benefit, to get a sense of spiritual superiority, to gain health, wealth, and prosperity, or to prove something to other people. They do not understand the principle of self-surrender and often end up discrediting the Holy Spirit.

—DOUG MCMURRY IN *THE PERSON AND WORK OF THE HOLY SPIRIT*

Nonstop Prayer

When the Spirit has come to reside in someone, that person cannot stop praying; for the Spirit prays without ceasing in him. No matter if he is asleep or awake, prayer is going on in his heart all the time. He may be eating or drinking, he may be resting or working—the incense of prayer will ascend spontaneously from his heart. The slightest stirring of his heart is like a voice which sings in silence and in secret to the Invisible.

—ISAAC THE SYRIAN

Good News

What does God do with the sins we confess to him? According to the Bible, God

- forgives and covers them (Psalm 32:1)
- does not count them against us (Psalm 32:2)
- removes them (Psalm 103:12)
- makes them white (Isaiah 1:18)
- blots them out of his memory (Isaiah 43:25)
- pardons them (Isaiah 55:7)
- hurls them into the sea (Micah 7:19)
- purifies us from them (1 John 1:9)
- puts them all behind his back (Isaiah 38:17)

If these are all true, we no longer have any reason to be afraid to talk to God about the times we have disobeyed him and hurt others or ourselves. He is always willing to listen and forgive if we are sorry for what we have done.

Christ already took our punishment for sin by dying in our place on the cross, so we don't have to fear God's anger. He loves us! We need only to accept his love and forgiveness, and to acknowledge him as Lord of our lives. This is good news!

Does Christ Live Here?

A new pastor had come to a village. One day he called at a certain cottage. When the husband came home from work, the wife said, "The new pastor called today."

"And what did he say?" asked the husband.

"He asked, 'Does Christ live here?' I didn't know what to answer."

With a flushed face, the husband asked, "Why didn't you tell him that we go to church and say our prayers and read our Bible?"

The wife replied, "He didn't ask me any of those things. He only asked, 'Does Christ live here?'"

Does Christ live in your home?

—BELMONT (N.C.) CHURCH BULLETIN

Spiritual Overdrive

The Holy Spirit, the third person of the Trinity, is the easiest of this not-at-all-easy concept for me to understand. Any artist, great or small, knows moments when something more than he takes over, and he moves into a kind of "overdrive," where he works as ordinarily he cannot work. When he is through, there is a sense of exhilaration, exhaustion, and joy. All our best work comes in this fashion, and it is humbling and exciting.

—MADELEINE L'ENGLE IN *THE IRRATIONAL SEASON*

What the Spirit Does

Jesus stays with us in the Spirit,
who renews our hearts,
moves us to faith,
leads us in the truth,
stands by us in our need,
and makes our obedience fresh and vibrant.

—*OUR WORLD BELONGS TO GOD*, STANZA 31

STUDY GUIDE

The Spirit as Our Counselor
Lesson 3

John 14:16-17, 25-26
¹⁶"I will ask the Father, and he will give you another Counselor to be with you forever—¹⁷the Spirit of truth. The world cannot accept him, because it neither sees him nor knows him. But you know him, for he lives with you and will be in you.

²⁵"All this I have spoken while still with you. ²⁶But the Counselor, the Holy Spirit, whom the Father will send in my name, will teach you all things and will remind you of everything I have said to you."

John 16:12-13
¹²"I have much more to say to you, more than you can now bear. ¹³But when he, the Spirit of truth, comes, he will guide you into all truth. He will not speak on his own; he will speak only what he hears, and he will tell you what is yet to come."

Matthew 10:18-20
¹⁸"On my account you will be brought before governors and kings as witnesses to them and to the Gentiles. ¹⁹But when they arrest you, do not worry about what to say or how to say it. At that time you will be given what to say, ²⁰for it will not be you speaking, but the Spirit of your Father speaking through you."

1 Corinthians 2:10-14, 16
¹⁰The Spirit searches all things, even the deep things of God. ¹¹For who among men knows the thoughts of a man except the man's spirit within him? In the same way no one knows the thoughts of God except the Spirit of God. ¹²We have not received the spirit of the world but the Spirit who is from God, that we may understand what God has freely given us. ¹³This is what we speak, not in words taught us by human wisdom but in words taught by the Spirit, expressing spiritual truths in spiritual words. ¹⁴The man without the Spirit does not accept the things that come from the Spirit of God, for they are foolishness to him, and he cannot understand them, because they are spiritually discerned. . . . ¹⁶But we have the mind of Christ.

Ephesians 1:17
¹⁷I keep asking that the God of our Lord Jesus Christ, the glorious Father, may give you the Spirit of wisdom and revelation, so that you may know him better.

Romans 8:26-27
²⁶In the same way, the Spirit helps us in our weakness. We do not know what we ought to pray for, but the Spirit himself intercedes for us with groans that words cannot express. ²⁷And he who searches our hearts knows the mind of the Spirit, because the Spirit intercedes for the saints in accordance with God's will.

Questions

1. What kinds of advisers—financial, business, medical—do you consult? Do you follow their advice as much as you should? Can you give an example?

2. John 14:16-17, 25-26
   a. What will the Father give to Jesus' followers?
   b. What will the Holy Spirit teach them?

3. John 16:12-13
   a. Why can't Jesus tell his followers everything they need to know at this point?
   b. What will the Spirit do for the believers?
   c. Why is that so important?

4. Matthew 10:18-20
   a. What does Jesus predict will happen to many of his followers?
   b. Why will they not need to worry?

5. 1 Corinthians 2:10-14, 16
   a. What does the Spirit know?
   b. What kinds of things does the Spirit teach believers?
   c. Why is it essential to receive God's Spirit in order to understand these things?
   d. Whose mind does the Spirit give to believers?

6. Ephesians 1:17
   a. How is the Holy Spirit described here?
   b. What will the Spirit enable the believers to do?

7. Romans 8:26-27
   a. In which other area does the Holy Spirit become our invaluable Counselor and help?
   b. What does the Spirit do for those who pray?

Summary
   a. What have you learned about the Holy Spirit in this lesson?
   b. How can you put that knowledge to use?

STUDIES IN THIS SERIES
Lesson 1: The Spirit Poured Out
Lesson 2: New Life in the Spirit
Lesson 3: The Spirit as Our Counselor
Lesson 4: The Spirit's Sword
Lesson 5: The Spirit of Holiness
Lesson 6: The Spirit of Power
Lesson 7: The Gifts of the Spirit

afterWord

The Spirit Helps When We Pray

The wonderful news I am trying to explain is this: while we are full participants in the grace-filled work of prayer, the work of prayer does not depend on us. We often pray in struggling, halting ways. Many times we have only fragmentary glimpses of the heavenly glory. We do not know what to pray. We do not know how to pray. Often our best prayers feel like inarticulate groans.

This is why the promise of Scripture comes as such good news: "The Spirit helps us in our weakness; for we do not know how to pray as we ought, but that very Spirit intercedes with sighs too deep for words. And God, who searches the heart, knows what is the mind of the Spirit, because the Spirit intercedes for the saints according to the will of God" (Romans 8:26-27).

Do you realize what a relief this is? The Holy Spirit of God, the third member of the Trinity, himself accompanies us in our prayers. When we stumble over our words, the Spirit straightens out the syntax. When we pray with muddy motives, the Spirit purifies the stream. When we see through a glass darkly, the Spirit adjusts and focuses what we are asking until it corresponds to the will of God.

The point is that we do not have to have everything perfect when we pray. The Spirit reshapes, refines, and reinterprets our feeble, ego-driven prayers. We can rest in this work of the Spirit on our behalf.

—RICHARD FOSTER IN *PRAYER*

A Deeper Power

Christ's kingdom is from heaven. It is not to be established by battles on earth. Muhammad launched his *jihad* with the sword; Jesus refused to take the sword or to allow his disciples to do so in his name. He refused even the sword of angels, for he could have summoned twelve legions of mighty ones (Matthew 26:53). Yet in withholding the sword Jesus did not withhold power. Even a cynical world that measures might by the megaton sees the convictions in people's minds break down walls of oppression. The collapse of Soviet communism demonstrated that once more. Yet the wind of the Spirit is not the power of ideology, but the deeper power of the Creator who makes all things new.

—EDMUND P. CLOWNEY IN *THE CHURCH*

The Holy Spirit Is a Person

The Holy Spirit performs personal tasks. The Holy Spirit relates to us as a person. He does things to us and for us, things that we normally associate with personal activity. He teaches us. He comforts us. He guides us. He encourages us.

These activities can be achieved at times by impersonal objects. Mariners can be "guided" by stars. We can take comfort by contemplating a beautiful sunset. But the comfort derived from such contemplation is based on a conscious or unconscious assumption that behind the sunset is a Personal Artist of the sunset. We can be "taught" by observing natural objects, but only by way of analogy.

The way in which the Spirit comforts, guides, teaches, etc., is a personal way. As He performs these tasks, the Bible describes His activity as involving intelligence, will, feeling, and power. The Spirit searches, selects, reveals, and admonishes. Stars and sunsets do not behave this way.

In summary, we conclude that if the Holy Spirit can be loved, adored, obeyed, offended, grieved, or sinned against, He must be a person.

—R. C. SPROUL IN *THE MYSTERY OF THE HOLY SPIRIT*

How to Get Out of Control

Before we can be filled with the Spirit ... we have to *give up control*. Submit. To anything and everything God has asked and might ask of us. In other words, *die to self*.

That in itself can be terrifying. Because most of us are more into control (or more accurately, *the attempt* to control) than we'd care to admit.

People who talk about the Holy Spirit can get pretty emotional, and that scares us. We don't want to look foolish. We're afraid of what might come to the surface if we dropped our guard and let the Spirit move as He wills.

We feel much more comfortable when *we* manage our Christian lives. Having marriage difficulties? Attend a conference. Struggling with besetting sins? Memorize a verse. Plagued by loneliness? Read a book on developing relationships, or join a singles' group. We like it a lot better when there's something *we* can do to solve our problems....

Guess what? Those who follow this pattern are destined for utter failure. Because love, joy, and all that other good stuff are the fruit *of the Spirit*, not the fruit of our efforts. We can't produce them on our own. Period. The fruit comes only as we submit our lives and let the *Spirit* control us.

Letting go of control is not easy, especially if we struggle with trusting God. I've been tremendously humbled in realizing that on my own, *I don't even have the ability to let go.* I am completely dependent on God even for that.... We have two choices: We can attempt to control our own lives with our own energy, or we can experience the rich, supernaturally powered life of being controlled by the Spirit. Not much of a choice, is it?

—SUSAN MAY / FEBRUARY 1996

STUDY GUIDE

Nov. 1 at Shirley

The Spirit's Sword
Lesson 4

Ephesians 6:11-12, 17
¹¹Put on the full armor of God so that you can take your stand against the devil's schemes. ¹²For our struggle is not against flesh and blood.... ¹⁷Take the helmet of salvation and the sword of the Spirit, which is the word of God.

Hebrews 4:12
¹²For the word of God is living and active. Sharper than any double-edged sword, it penetrates even to dividing soul and spirit, joints and marrow; it judges the thoughts and attitudes of the heart.

2 Timothy 3:16-17
¹⁶All Scripture is God-breathed and is useful for teaching, rebuking, correcting and training in righteousness, ¹⁷so that the man of God may be thoroughly equipped for every good work.

2 Peter 1:19-21
¹⁹And we have the word of the prophets made more certain, and you will do well to pay attention to it, as to a light shining in a dark place ... ²⁰Above all, you must understand that no prophecy of Scripture came about by the prophet's own interpretation. ²¹For prophecy never had its origin in the will of man, but men spoke from God as they were carried along by the Holy Spirit.

1 Peter 1:10-12
¹⁰Concerning this salvation, the prophets, who spoke of the grace that was to come to you, searched intently and with the greatest care, ¹¹trying to find out the time and circumstances to which the Spirit of Christ in them was pointing when he predicted the sufferings of Christ and the glories that would follow. ¹²It was revealed to them that they were not serving themselves but you, when they spoke of the things that have now been told you by those who have preached the gospel to you by the Holy Spirit sent from heaven. Even angels long to look into these things.

Romans 15:4, 13
⁴For everything that was written in the past was written to teach us, so that through endurance and the encouragement of the Scriptures we might have hope.... ¹³May the God of hope fill you with all joy and peace as you trust in him, so that you may overflow with hope by the power of the Holy Spirit.

Questions

1. Can you give an example of a book or a speech that made a great impact in your life? What happened?

2. Ephesians 6:11-12, 17
   a. What kind of battle do you think believers are engaged in?
   b. Who provides the armor for this battle?
   c. In New Testament times what purpose did a sword serve? How important was it in battle?

3. Hebrews 4:12
   a. How is the Bible different from any other book?
   b. How does the Holy Spirit use it in people's lives?

4. 2 Timothy 3:16-17
   a. What word does Paul use to describe Scripture?
   b. What specific uses of Scripture does Paul list?

5. 2 Peter 1:19-21
   a. What should believers be paying attention to?
   b. What is the origin of every prophecy of Scripture?

6. 1 Peter 1:10-12
   a. How did the Old Testament prophets respond to these glimpses of the coming Christ?
   b. How did the Spirit answer their questioning?

7. Romans 15:4, 13
   a. Why were the Scriptures preserved in written form?
   b. What fills believers as they study the Scriptures?

Summary
What have you learned about the relationship between the Holy Spirit and the Bible?

STUDIES IN THIS SERIES

Lesson 1: The Spirit Poured Out
Lesson 2: New Life in the Spirit
Lesson 3: The Spirit as Our Counselor
Lesson 4: The Spirit's Sword
Lesson 5: The Spirit of Holiness
Lesson 6: The Spirit of Power
Lesson 7: The Gifts of the Spirit

afterWord

A Window on the Word

Famed evangelist Dwight L. Moody recalled a visit to Baltimore. "My window looked out on an Episcopal church. The stained-glass windows were dull and uninviting by day, but when the lights shone through at night, how beautiful they were!

"So when the Holy Spirit touches the eyes of your understanding and you see Christ shining through the pages of the Bible, it becomes a new book."

The Greatest Communicator

The Spirit was and is the agent of all communication from God. Both the giving and the receiving of revelation are his work. The reason why it can be said that "the spirit of man is the lamp of the Lord . . ." (Proverbs 20:27) is not that we pick up divine truth naturally, without special divine help, as some have supposed; the reason is that the Holy Spirit brings revealed truth home to our otherwise impervious hearts. In other words, the spirit of man is a lamp that is out till the Holy Spirit lights it.

—J. I. PACKER IN *KEEP IN STEP WITH THE SPIRIT*

The Written Word of God

We confess that this Word of God was not sent nor delivered by the will of men, but that holy men of God spoke, being moved by the Holy Spirit, as Peter says.

Afterwards our God—because of the special care he has for us and our salvation—commanded his servants, the prophets and apostles, to commit this revealed Word to writing. He himself wrote with his own finger the two tables of the law.

Therefore we call such writings holy and divine Scriptures.

—THE BELGIC CONFESSION, ARTICLE 3

God Has Spoken

God has not left this world
without ways of knowing him.
He shows his power and majesty
in the creation;
he has mercifully spoken
through prophets, history writers, poets,
gospel writers, and apostles—
and most clearly through the Son.
The Spirit who moved humans
to write the Word of God
speaks to us in the Bible.

—OUR WORLD BELONGS TO GOD, STANZA 34

Inspired Words

Ever since Satan questioned Eve in the Garden of Eden, "Indeed, has God said . . . ," men have attacked the Word of God. But every time in history they have doubted it, dire consequences have resulted—whether in the life of an individual, a nation (ancient Israel), or the Church. Without exception the individual, the nation, or the Church went into a period of spiritual decline. Often idolatry and immorality followed.

Competent scholars agree that the Holy Spirit did not merely use the biblical writers as secretaries to whom He dictated the Scriptures, although some sincere Christians think He did this. The Bible itself does not state in detail just *how* the Holy Spirit accomplished His purpose in getting the Scripture written. However, we do know that He used living human minds and guided their thoughts according to His divine purposes. Moreover, it has always been clear to me that we cannot have inspired ideas without inspired words.

—BILLY GRAHAM IN *THE HOLY SPIRIT*

The Unrivaled Power of Prayer

We realize that we are energized by the Holy Spirit for prayer; we know what it is to pray in the Spirit; but we do not so often realize that the Holy Spirit Himself prays in us prayers which we cannot utter. When we are born again of God and are indwelt by the Spirit of God, He expresses for us the unutterable.

"He," the Spirit in you, "maketh intercession for the saints according to the will of God," and God searches your heart not to know what your conscious prayers are, but to find out what is the prayer of the Holy Spirit.

The Spirit of God needs the nature of the believer as a shrine in which to offer His intercession. "Your body is the temple of the Holy Ghost." When Jesus Christ cleansed the temple, He "would not suffer that any man should carry any vessel through the temple." The Spirit of God will not allow you to use your body for your own convenience. Jesus ruthlessly cast out all them that sold and bought in the temple, and said—"My house shall be called the house of prayer; but ye have made it a den of thieves."

Have we recognized that our body is the temple of the Holy Ghost? If so, we must be careful to keep it undefiled for Him. We have to remember that our conscious life, though it is only a tiny bit of our personality, is to be regarded by us as a shrine of the Holy Ghost. He will look after the unconscious part that we know nothing of; but we must see that we guard the conscious part for which we are responsible.

—OSWALD CHAMBERS IN *MY UTMOST FOR HIS HIGHEST*

STUDY GUIDE

The Spirit of Holiness
Lesson 5

1 Corinthians 6:9-11
⁹Do you not know that the wicked will not inherit the kingdom of God? Do not be deceived: Neither the sexually immoral nor idolaters nor adulterers nor male prostitutes nor homosexual offenders ¹⁰nor thieves nor the greedy nor drunkards nor slanderers nor swindlers will inherit the kingdom of God. ¹¹And that is what some of you were. But you were washed, you were sanctified, you were justified in the name of the Lord Jesus Christ and by the Spirit of our God.

Titus 3:3-6
³At one time we too were foolish, disobedient, deceived and enslaved by all kinds of passions and pleasures. We lived in malice and envy, being hated and hating one another. ⁴But when the kindness and love of God our Savior appeared, ⁵he saved us, not because of righteous things we had done, but because of his mercy. He saved us through the washing of rebirth and renewal by the Holy Spirit, ⁶whom he poured out on us generously through Jesus Christ our Savior.

Galatians 5:22-25
²²But the fruit of the Spirit is love, joy, peace, patience, kindness, goodness, faithfulness, ²³gentleness and self-control. Against such things there is no law. ²⁴Those who belong to Christ Jesus have crucified the sinful nature with its passions and desires. ²⁵Since we live by the Spirit, let us keep in step with the Spirit.

1 Corinthians 6:18-19
¹⁸Flee from sexual immorality. All other sins a man commits are outside his body, but he who sins sexually sins against his own body. ¹⁹Do you not know that your body is a temple of the Holy Spirit, who is in you, whom you have received from God?

Ephesians 4:30-32
³⁰Do not grieve the Holy Spirit of God, with whom you were sealed for the day of redemption. ³¹Get rid of all bitterness, rage and anger, brawling and slander, along with every form of malice. ³²Be kind and compassionate to one another, forgiving each other, just as in Christ God forgave you.

2 Corinthians 3:17-18
¹⁷Now the Lord is the Spirit, and where the Spirit of the Lord is, there is freedom. ¹⁸And we, who with unveiled faces all reflect the Lord's glory, are being transformed into his likeness with ever-increasing glory, which comes from the Lord, who is the Spirit.

STUDIES IN THIS SERIES
Lesson 1: The Spirit Poured Out
Lesson 2: New Life in the Spirit
Lesson 3: The Spirit as Our Counselor
Lesson 4: The Spirit's Sword
Lesson 5: The Spirit of Holiness
Lesson 6: The Spirit of Power
Lesson 7: The Gifts of the Spirit

Questions

1. What kinds of things make it hard for you to live a clean, pure life?

2. 1 Corinthians 6:9-11
   a. Who will not inherit the kingdom of God?
   b. What kind of life did some of the believers at Corinth lead?
   c. What happened to these people "by the Spirit of our God"?

3. Titus 3:3-6
   a. What are many people's lives like before they are saved by God's kindness?
   b. For what reason does God save them?
   c. What is the Holy Spirit's role in this?

4. Galatians 5:22-25
   a. What is the fruit of new life in the Spirit?
   b. How does this contrast with the way of life described in the two earlier passages?
   c. What do believers do with their sinful nature?

5. 1 Corinthians 6:18-19
   a. What is particularly wrong with sexual sin?
   b. What is very special about the physical body of a believer?

6. Ephesians 4:30-32
   a. What kinds of things grieve the Holy Spirit?
   b. Who are Spirit-filled believers supposed to imitate?

7. 2 Corinthians 3:17-18
   a. What do believers find in the presence of God's Spirit?
   b. What transformation does the Spirit bring into their lives?

Summary
   a. What characterizes the lives of those who are filled with the Holy Spirit?
   b. How do they differ from other people?

afterWord

What Is Holiness?

Holiness is the fruit of the Spirit, displayed as the Christian walks by the Spirit (Galatians 5:16, 22, 25). Holiness is consecrated closeness to God. Holiness is in essence obeying God, living to God and for God, imitating God, keeping his law, taking his side against sin, doing righteousness, performing good works, following Christ's teaching and example, worshiping God in the Spirit, loving and serving God and men out of reverence for Christ.

In relation to God, holiness takes the form of a single-minded passion to please by love and loyalty, devotion, and praise. In relation to sin, it takes the form of a resistance movement, a discipline of not gratifying the desires of the flesh, but of putting to death the deeds of the body (Galatians 5:16; Romans 8:13). Holiness is, in a word, God-taught, Spirit-wrought Christ-likeness, the sum and substance of committed discipleship, the demonstration of faith working by love, the responsive outflow in righteousness of supernatural life from the hearts of those who are born again.

—J. I. PACKER IN *KEEP IN STEP WITH THE SPIRIT*

Saved to Holiness

The third person of the Trinity is named the Holy Spirit. We wonder why the title *Holy* is ascribed in a special way to Him. The attribute of holiness belongs to the Father and to the Son as well. Yet we normally do not speak of the Trinity in terms of the Holy Father, the Holy Son, and the Holy Spirit.

Though the Spirit is no more and no less holy than the Father and the Son, the *Holy* in His name calls attention to the focal point of His work in the [plan] of redemption. The Holy Spirit is the Sanctifier. He is the One who applies the work of Christ to our lives by working in us to bring us to full conformity and the image of Christ.

In salvation we are not only saved from sin and damnation; we are saved unto holiness. The goal of redemption is holiness.

—R. C. SPROUL IN *THE MYSTERY OF THE HOLY SPIRIT*

Filthy Clothes, Rich Garments

One warm, muddy spring night I tramped across lawns and meadows to visit my fiancee, who was living with her grandparents. They greeted me with surprise and ushered me into the living room.

Suddenly they glanced at my feet. I looked down. Particles of mud had fallen onto their immaculate, cream-colored carpet from the treads on my boots. I looked back toward the door. There was a trail of mud from the door to where I was sitting.

They did not say a word, merely stood up and got the broom and dustpan. I felt embarrassed, ashamed, and guilty. Even now, twenty-five years later, I feel the sting of that disgrace.

A few months ago, in an all-day committee meeting, I spilled spaghetti sauce on my white dress shirt. It would not wash out, and I sat through the rest of the meeting feeling embarrassed and self-conscious. I felt as though my stained clothes were shouting, "Messy eater!"

Dirty clothes can do that to us. They make us feel ashamed and self-conscious. The Bible uses this picture to express how even believers feel when standing before God's holiness. All our mistakes and sins feel like dirty, embarrassing clothes—and Satan, our great Accuser, is standing behind us, pointing out to God those particularly dirty stains.

A stain comes quickly, easily. One mistake, one slip into sin, feels like an embarrassing stain. It can make us cringe for the rest of the day—or the rest of our lives. And Satan takes every opportunity to remind us of our stains.

But God takes drastic measures. He takes off our filthy clothes. Then he puts on "rich garments." Or, as the book of Revelation puts it, "fine linen, bright and clean." Those who wear these white clothes "have washed their robes and made them white in the blood of the Lamb" (Revelation 7:14).

The next time you sin, the next time you hear Satan's voice accusing you of things you've done wrong, do this exercise in spiritual imagination. First, step out of those filthy clothes. Then wash them in Jesus' blood. Pull them out, white and shining, and put them on. Now stand before God, before the angels, and before the great Accuser—clothed in rich, clean garments.

"Come now, let us reason together," says the Lord. "Though your sins are like scarlet, they shall be as white as snow."

—ANONYMOUS

How to Grow with the Spirit

Many people have a quite negative conception of Christianity, as if it consisted in continual self-amputation, as if God wanted to hold us down, rather than that we should "turn again and live." Would such a God deserve the name of Father which Christ gave to him? When I labour to liberate a crushed life, I am not fighting against God, but with him. Like a gardener who removes from around a plant the weeds that choke it, using all the care that as one of God's creatures it deserves, I am helping to reestablish his purpose of life. It is God who gave it life, and he surely wants it to flourish and bear fruit. Does not Christ often speak of bearing fruit? Bearing fruit means being oneself, asserting oneself, growing in accordance with God's purpose.

Christianity, therefore, has its positive, affirmative, creative aspect—ignored by many Christians. I do not deny that it imposes certain specific acts of renunciation. Jesus spoke of the husbandman who prunes his vine so that it may bear more fruit. The purpose of pruning is not to restrict life, but on the contrary to promote its fuller and richer flow.

—PAUL TOURNIER IN *THE MEANING OF PERSONS*

STUDY GUIDE

The Spirit of Power
Lesson 6

Luke 3:21-22; 4:14

²¹When all the people were being baptized, Jesus was baptized too. And as he was praying, heaven was opened ²²and the Holy Spirit descended on him in bodily form like a dove. And a voice came from heaven: "You are my Son, whom I love; with you I am well pleased."

¹⁴Jesus returned to Galilee in the power of the Spirit, and news about him spread through the whole countryside.

Isaiah 11:2

²The Spirit of the Lord will rest on him—
the Spirit of wisdom and of understanding,
the Spirit of counsel and of power . . .

Luke 24:46, 49

⁴⁶[Jesus] told them, . . . ⁴⁹"I am going to send you what my Father has promised; but stay in the city until you have been clothed with power from on high."

Acts 1:8

⁸"You will receive power when the Holy Spirit comes on you; and you will be my witnesses in Jerusalem, and in all Judea and Samaria, and to the ends of the earth."

1 Corinthians 2:1-5

¹When I came to you, brothers, I did not come with eloquence or superior wisdom as I proclaimed to you the testimony about God. ²For I resolved to know nothing while I was with you except Jesus Christ and him crucified. ³I came to you in weakness and fear, and with much trembling. ⁴My message and my preaching were not with wise and persuasive words, but with a demonstration of the Spirit's power, ⁵so that your faith might not rest on men's wisdom, but on God's power.

Ephesians 3:16, 20-21

¹⁶I pray that out of [the Father's] glorious riches he may strengthen you with power through his Spirit in your inner being. . . . ²⁰Now to him who is able to do immeasurably more than all that we ask or imagine, according to his power that is at work within us, ²¹to him be glory in the church and in Christ Jesus throughout all generations, for ever and ever! Amen.

Ephesians 6:10-12

¹⁰Finally, be strong in the Lord and in his mighty power. ¹¹Put on the full armor of God so that you can take your stand against the devil's schemes. ¹²For our struggle is not against flesh and blood, but against the rulers, against the authorities, against the powers of this dark world and against the spiritual forces of evil in the heavenly realms.

STUDIES IN THIS SERIES

Lesson 1: The Spirit Poured Out
Lesson 2: New Life in the Spirit
Lesson 3: The Spirit as Our Counselor
Lesson 4: The Spirit's Sword
Lesson 5: The Spirit of Holiness
Lesson 6: The Spirit of Power
Lesson 7: The Gifts of the Spirit

Questions

1. Have you ever faced a task or challenge that you knew you had to do—but also knew you couldn't do in your own strength?

2. **Luke 3:21-22; 4:14**
   a. What happens when Jesus is being baptized?
   b. How does this prepare Jesus for his ministry?

3. **Isaiah 11:2**
   a. How is this prophecy fulfilled in Jesus' life?
   b. What qualities does Jesus receive as a result?

4. **Luke 24:46, 49**
   What does Jesus want his followers to wait for?

5. **Acts 1:8**
   a. What needed quality does the Holy Spirit give to Jesus' followers?
   b. What will it enable them to become?

6. **1 Corinthians 2:1-5**
   a. How does Paul describe his preaching and teaching? What does he say was lacking?
   b. What made Paul's speaking so effective?

7. **Ephesians 3:16, 20-21**
   a. What gift does Paul ask God to give the believers?
   b. How great is the power of God's Spirit that is at work within believers?

8. **Ephesians 6:10-12**
   a. Whose strength do believers need to seek? Why?
   b. In what kind of struggle is this power needed?

Summary
   a. What tremendous resource is offered to believers through the indwelling of the Holy Spirit?
   b. What happens to believers who ignore this resource?

afterWord

Huffing and Puffing

Spirit, like all biblical terms that refer to God, is a picture-word with a vivid, precise, and colorful meaning. It pictures breath breathed or panted out, as when you blow out the candles on your birthday cake or blow up balloons or puff and blow as you run. *Spirit* in this sense was what the big bad wolf was threatening the little pigs with when he told them, "I'll huff, and I'll puff, and I'll blow your house down!" The picture is of air made to move vigorously, even violently, and the thought that the picture expresses is of energy let loose, executive force invading, power in exercise, life demonstrated by activity.... Power in action is in fact the basic biblical thought whenever God's Spirit is mentioned.

—J. I. PACKER IN *KEEP IN STEP WITH THE SPIRIT*

Moody's Legacy

Dwight L. Moody's influence continues to bless the whole body of Christ a full century after his height of ministry. The Moody Church in Chicago, Moody Bible Institute, the Moody Radio Network and Moody Press all are a continued outflowing of a river of mightiness that began in the soul of this one man—passionate for God. He describes the pathway by which he came to his own "anointing" or "filling" (his words) with the Holy Spirit.

He had begun to be awakened to his need through a brief, momentary contact with an aged man whom he met one day following a service in New York. The gray-haired saint touched Moody's shoulder and, as the evangelist turned to look into his eyes, spoke these earnest, pointed words: "Young man, when you speak again, honor the Holy Ghost." Moody elaborates this poignant dealing of the Lord, linking it to the prayers and personal words of encouragement he received from two godly women in his congregation. They had gently spoken to him of their praying for his "anointing for special service."

"You need power," they urged their pastor, yet not without respect.

Moody confides his inner thoughts at the time.

"I need power?' I said to myself. 'Why, I thought I had power. I had a large Sabbath school, and the largest congregation in Chicago. There were *some* conversions at the time, and I was in a sense satisfied."

He describes the awakening of his own passion for fullness. "There came a great hunger into my soul. I knew not what it was. I began to cry as never before. The hunger increased. I really felt that I did not want to live any longer if I could not have this power for service. I kept on crying all the time that God would fill me with His Spirit."

While in New York, seeking help for victims of the great Chicago fire of 1871, which destroyed a third of the city, Moody's quest was answered. He says, "My heart was not in the work of begging. I could not appeal. I was crying all the time that God would fill me with His Spirit. Well, one day, in the city of New York—oh, what a day!—I cannot describe it. I seldom refer to it; it is almost too sacred an experience to name. Paul had an experience of which he didn't speak for fourteen years. I can only say that God revealed Himself to me, and I had such an experience of His love that I had to ask Him to stay his hand.

"I went to preaching again. The sermons were not different; I did not present any new truths, and yet hundreds were converted. I would not now be placed back where I was before that blessed experience if you should give me all the world—it would be as the small dust of the balance."

—JACK HAYFORD IN *A PASSION FOR FULLNESS*

Sin Needs an Inside Job

We are accustomed to thinking of sin as individual acts of disobedience to God. That is true enough as far as it goes, but Scripture goes much farther. In Romans the apostle Paul frequently referred to sin as a condition that plagues the human race. Sin as a condition works its way out through the "bodily members"; that is, the ingrained habits of the body. And there is no slavery that can compare to the slavery of ingrained habits of sin....

Sin is part of the internal structure of our lives. No special effort is needed. No wonder we feel trapped.

Our ordinary method of dealing with ingrained sin is to launch a frontal attack. We rely on our willpower and determination. Whatever the issue for us may be—anger, bitterness, gluttony, pride, sexual lust, alcohol, fear—we determine never to do it again; we pray against it, fight against it, set our will against it. But it is all vain, and we find ourselves once again morally bankrupt or, worse yet, so proud of our external righteousness that "whitened sepulchers" is a mild description of our condition....

Willpower has no defense against the careless word, the unguarded moment. The will has the same deficiency as the law—it can deal only with externals. It is not sufficient to bring about the necessary transformation of the inner spirit.

When we despair of gaining inner transformation through human powers of will and determination, we are open to a wonderful new realization: inner righteousness is a gift from God to be graciously received. The needed change within us is God's work, not ours. The demand is for an inside job, and only God can work from the inside.

—RICHARD FOSTER IN *CELEBRATION OF DISCIPLINE*

STUDY GUIDE

The Gifts of the Spirit
Lesson 7

Hebrews 2:3-4

³This salvation, which was first announced by the Lord, was confirmed to us by those who heard him. ⁴God also testified to it by signs, wonders and various miracles, and gifts of the Holy Spirit distributed according to his will.

1 Corinthians 12:1, 4-11

¹Now about spiritual gifts, brothers, I do not want you to be ignorant.... ⁴There are different kinds of gifts, but the same Spirit. ⁵There are different kinds of service, but the same Lord. ⁶There are different kinds of working, but the same God works all of them in all men.

⁷Now to each one the manifestation of the Spirit is given for the common good. ⁸To one there is given through the Spirit the message of wisdom, to another the message of knowledge by means of the same Spirit, ⁹to another faith by the same Spirit, to another gifts of healing by that one Spirit, ¹⁰to another miraculous powers, to another prophecy, to another distinguishing between spirits, to another speaking in different kinds of tongues, and to still another the interpretation of tongues. ¹¹All these are the work of one and the same Spirit, and he gives them to each one, just as he determines.

1 Corinthians 12:12-13, 27-31

¹²The body is a unit, though it is made up of many parts; and though all its parts are many, they form one body. So it is with Christ. ¹³For we were all baptized by one Spirit into one body—whether Jews or Greeks, slave or free—and we were all given the one Spirit to drink....

²⁷Now you are the body of Christ, and each one of you is a part of it. ²⁸And in the church God has appointed first of all apostles, second prophets, third teachers, then workers of miracles, also those having gifts of healing, those able to help others, those with gifts of administration, and those speaking in different kinds of tongues. ²⁹Are all apostles? Are all prophets? Are all teachers? Do all work miracles? ³⁰Do all have gifts of healing? Do all speak in tongues? Do all interpret? ³¹But eagerly desire the greater gifts.

Romans 12:3, 6-8

³For by the grace given me I say to every one of you: Do not think of yourself more highly than you ought, but rather think of yourself with sober judgment, in accordance with the measure of faith God has given you....

⁶We have different gifts, according to the grace given us. If a man's gift is prophesying, let him use it in proportion to his faith. ⁷If it is serving, let him serve; it if is teaching, let him teach; ⁸if it is encouraging, let him encourage; if it is contributing to the needs of others, let him give generously; if it is leadership, let him govern diligently; if it is showing mercy, let him do it cheerfully.

1 Corinthians 14:1, 3, 12

¹Follow the way of love and eagerly desire spiritual gifts, especially the gift of prophecy.... ³Everyone who prophesies speaks to men for their strengthening, encouragement and comfort.... ¹²Since you are eager to have spiritual gifts, try to excel in gifts that build up the church.

STUDIES IN THIS SERIES

Lesson 1: The Spirit Poured Out
Lesson 2: New Life in the Spirit
Lesson 3: The Spirit as Our Counselor
Lesson 4: The Spirit's Sword
Lesson 5: The Spirit of Holiness
Lesson 6: The Spirit of Power
Lesson 7: The Gifts of the Spirit

Questions

1. What is one thing you do really well? How does that one ability make you feel?

2. **Hebrews 2:3-4**
   a. Would you be impressed by someone's message if it were accompanied by signs, wonders, and various miracles? Explain.
   b. What does God distribute to believers through the Holy Spirit? For what purpose?

3. **1 Corinthians 12:1, 4-11**
   a. What point do these verses make about the Holy Spirit?
   b. Why is each believer given a "manifestation" of the Holy Spirit?
   c. How can each of the spiritual gifts listed be used for the common good in God's family?

4. **1 Corinthians 12:12-13, 27-31**
   a. How do these verses describe the body of Christ?
   b. How does the list of spiritual gifts here compare to that of the previous passage?
   c. Which seem to be the greater gifts? Why?

5. **Romans 12:3, 6-8**
   a. How should someone who is a member of Christ's body think about himself or herself?
   b. What gifts are mentioned here that have not been mentioned in previous passages?
   c. How is each gift to be used?

6. **1 Corinthians 14:1, 3, 12**
   a. According to this passage, what should be our attitude toward spiritual gifts?
   b. What is one of the greatest spiritual gifts? Why?
   c. Which gifts should believers try to excel in?

Summary

According to the Scripture passages in this lesson, what should the church be like?

*after*Word

Body or Bus?

The fact that every Christian has a gift and therefore a responsibility . . . should transform the life of Christians and of churches. For the traditional image of the local church is of an overworked pastor, assisted perhaps by a small nucleus of dedicated workers, while the majority of members make little or no contribution to the church's life and work. It conjures up the picture of a bus (one driver, many drowsy passengers) rather than of a body (all members active, each contributing a particular activity to the health and effectiveness of the whole).

—JOHN R. W. STOTT IN *BAPTISM AND FULLNESS*

Faking It

There is a counterfeit olive tree in Palestine. It is called the wild olive, or the oleander. It is in all points like the genuine tree, except that it yields no fruit. When I see a person taking up a large space in Christ's spiritual orchard and absorbing a vast amount of sunlight and soil and yielding no real fruit, I say, "Ah, there is an oleander."

—*ENCYCLOPEDIA OF SERMON ILLUSTRATIONS*

Grieving the Spirit

One day several friends and I were discussing major changes in my former church. I made a somewhat derogatory comment about a church leader. Suddenly I felt a "lurch" in my spirit, as if something inside me had been ripped away. I knew I'd offended the Spirit, and that He had withdrawn to some far-off corner of my heart. I'd grieved the Spirit in the past, but the intensity of my remorse was new to me. I was sickened by my words, horrified by my arrogance, and saddened that I had hurt the One I loved.

I was grateful for the churning within me. It is impossible to understand grieving the Spirit from a strictly cognitive perspective. Grieving involves deep emotion. The Spirit's sorrow had become my sorrow. I hated sin with a new vengeance and resolved to know the things that grieved the Spirit so I could avoid hurting Him in the future.

—LORRAINE PINTUS IN *DISCIPLESHIP JOURNAL*, JANUARY/FEBRUARY 1996

The Purpose of Gifts

The possession of gifts for service in Christ's church constitutes a call for their use. We are not to wrap our gifts in a napkin and bury them (Luke 19:20). Stewards (servant managers) must be trustworthy. We use our gifts in order to serve God, not in order to advance ourselves, attract the admiration of others, or even find satisfaction and fulfillment. We cannot demand that the Lord provide precisely the socket into which our gifts may best be plugged. Our first goal is to get the job done, and only secondarily to find the best use of our gifts. To be sure, the Lord who calls us will provide opportunities for the use of the gifts he has given. Paul sought open doors of gospel witness and urged Christians to do the same, "buying up" the opportunities that God provided (Ephesians 5:16).

—EDMUND P. CLOWNEY IN *THE CHURCH*

The Christian's Real Sin

[The fruits of the Spirit] are there to flow out through the agency of the Holy Spirit through us into the external world. The fruits are normal; not to have them is not to have the Christian life which should be considered usual. There are oceans of grace which wait. Orchard upon orchard waits, vineyard upon vineyard of fruit waits. There is only one reason why they do not flow out through the Christian's life, and that is that the instrumentality of faith is not being used. This is to quench the Holy Spirit. When we sin in this sense, we . . . have not raised the empty hands of faith for the gift that is there.

In the light of the structure of the total universe; in the light of our calling to exhibit the existence and character of God between the ascension and the second coming; in the light of the terrible price of the cross, whereby all the present and future benefits of salvation were purchased on our behalf—in the light of all this, the real sin of the Christian is not to possess his possessions, by faith. This is the real sin.

—FRANCIS SCHAEFFER IN *TRUE SPIRITUALITY*

THE HOLY SPIRIT: UNDER THE INFLUENCE

Evaluation Questionnaire

As you complete this study, we invite you to fill out this questionnaire to help us evaluate the effectiveness of our materials. Please be candid.

1. What church or denomination are you from?

2. Where did the group meet? How large was the group? What was the average age of your group?

3. Was this a church group?___ Mostly unchurched?___ A mix of church and unchurched?___

4. How would you rate the materials?

    Study Guide:
    ___ excellent ___ very good ___ good ___ fair ___ poor

    Leader's Guide:
    ___ excellent ___ very good ___ good ___ fair ___ poor

5. What did you like best about the materials? Did you like the format of the materials? Comment?

6. What would you do to improve the materials?

7. In general, what was the experience of the group?

8. How can we help you in the future?

Other comments:

(Optional) Your name _____

Address _____

Fold and tape to mail.

Place
Stamp
Here

FAITH ALIVE CHRISTIAN RESOURCES
2850 KALAMAZOO AVENUE SE
GRAND RAPIDS, MI 49560-0300

Fold and tape to mail.